Amazing Trees

Catherine Baker

RIGBY

Contents

Amazing Sizes	4
Amazing Shapes	8
Amazing Colours	14
Amazing Trees	20
Glossary	24

Amazing Sizes

Trees can be big or small.
Some trees are very big.

Here are some very tall trees. The people look very small.

This tree is very wide.

Some trees are so big you can sit in them!

Some trees are very small. This tree is so small that you can pick it up!

Here are some very small trees.
They are growing at a tree farm.

Amazing Shapes

Trees can be lots of shapes. Some trees have a spiky shape.

This tree grows in the desert.

This tree is very spiky.

The trees in this forest have long, thin shapes.

This is a pine forest.

All of these trees look like triangles.

These trees will all be Christmas trees!

This is a palm tree.
It has an amazing shape.

These trees look amazing in the snow!

The ice and snow make amazing shapes.

twig

icicles

Old trees can have amazing shapes, too.

This old tree is in a desert.

Amazing Colours

Leaves can have lots of amazing colours.

These maple leaves are bright red and yellow.

Here are some trees with bright yellow leaves.

These leaves are lots of bright colours.

Some trees have flowers with amazing colours.

These bright pink flowers are from an apple tree.

This is a cherry tree. Its flowers are pink too.

Some trees have fruit. The fruit can be lots of colours.

peach

orange

Fruit can be bright orange.

Fruit can be yellow, red or purple!

These bananas are bright yellow.

This is a big red apple.

These plums are purple.

Amazing Trees

Trees can be lots of fun! You can swing from a tree.

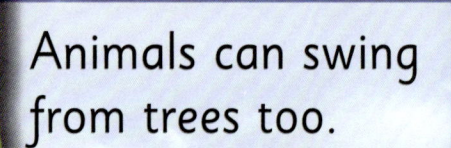

Animals can swing from trees too.

You can play in a tree.

Animals can play in trees too.

You can hide in a tree.

Animals can hide in trees too.

You can have a house in a tree.

Birds can have tree houses too!

Glossary

apple

bananas

cherry tree

flowers

icicles

leaves

maple

orange

palm tree

peach

plums

tree house